INSIDE THE NFL

BALTIMORE RAVENS

by Luke Hanlon

Abdo & Daughters
MIDDLE GRADE NONFICTION

An imprint of Abdo Publishing
abdobooks.com

ABDOBOOKS.COM

Published by Abdo Publishing, a division of ABDO, PO Box 398166, Minneapolis, Minnesota 55439.

Printed in China.
052025
092025

Cover Photos: Andy Lyons/Getty Images Sport/Getty Images (Lamar Jackson); David Madison/Getty Images Sport/Getty Images (Ray Lewis)
Interior Photos: Michael Reaves/Getty Images Sport/Getty Images, 4–5, 9, 11, 63; Eric Espada/Getty Images Sport/Getty Images, 6; Tom Pennington/Getty Images Sport/Getty Images, 7, 61 (bottom right); Rob Carr/Getty Images Sport/Getty Images, 8, 56–57, 61 (top right); Wilfredo Lee/AP Images, 10; Abdo Publishing, 12–13, 58; Focus on Sport/Getty Images Sport/Getty Images, 14–15; Lloyd Pearson/The Baltimore Sun/AP Images, 16; George Gojkovich/Getty Images Sport/Getty Images, 17, 21 (top); Mitchell Layton/Getty Images Sport/Getty Images, 18, 31; Wally Santana/AP Images, 19; Dave Hammond/AP Images, 20 (top), 60 (bottom left); Four Seam Images/AP Images, 20 (bottom); Bill Kostroun/AP Images, 21 (bottom); Michael J. Minardi/Getty Images Sport/Getty Images, 22–23; Mark Humphrey/AP Images, 24; Harry How/Allsport/Getty Images Sport/Getty Images, 25, 60 (bottom right); Neil Brake/AFP/Getty Images, 26; Jeff Haynes/AFP/Getty Images, 27; Rick Bowmer/AP Images, 28, 60 (top left); Andy Lyons/Getty Images Sport/Getty Images, 30; David Maxwell/Getty Images Sport/Getty Images, 32 (top); Dilip Vishwanat/Getty Images Sport Classic/Getty Images, 32 (bottom); Jamie Squire/Getty Images Sport/Getty Images, 33, 43, 48; Rob Carr/AP Images, 34–35, 60 (top right); Nick Laham/Getty Images Sport/Getty Images, 36–37, 39; Joe Robbins/AP Images, 38; Elsa/Getty Images Sport/Getty Images, 41, 61 (top left); Greg Trott/AP Images, 42 (top); Perry Knotts/AP Images, 42 (bottom); Ezra Shaw/Getty Images Sport/Getty Images, 44; Christian Petersen/Getty Images Sport/Getty Images, 45, 61 (bottom left); Chris Graythen/Getty Images Sport/Getty Images, 46–47; Jason Miller/Getty Images Sport/Getty Images, 49; Bryan Woolston/Getty Images Sport/Getty Images, 50; Will Newton/Getty Images Sport/Getty Images, 51; Wesley Hitt/Getty Images Sport/Getty Images, 52; Rick Osentoski/AP Images, 53; Patrick Smith/Getty Images Sport/Getty Images, 54, 59; Robin Alam/Icon Sportswire/Getty Images, 55

Editor: Haley Williams
Series Designer: Laura Graphenteen
Production Designer: Ebonee Estrella

Library of Congress Control Number: 2024948484

Publisher's Cataloging-in-Publication Data

Names: Hanlon, Luke, author.
Title: Baltimore Ravens / by Luke Hanlon
Description: Minneapolis, Minnesota: Abdo Publishing, 2026 | Series: Inside the NFL | Includes online resources and index.
Identifiers: ISBN 9781098296643 (lib. bdg.) | ISBN 9798384919162 (ebook)
Subjects: LCSH: Baltimore Ravens (Football team)--Juvenile literature. | National Football League--Juvenile literature. | Football teams--Juvenile literature. | American football--Juvenile literature.
Classification: DDC 796.333--dc23

CONTENTS

Baltimore Ravens quarterback Lamar Jackson was 22 years old at the start of the 2019 season.

CHAPTER 1

AIRING IT OUT

LINED UP IN THE SHOTGUN FORMATION, LAMAR JACKSON TOOK THE SNAP and quickly got to work. The Baltimore Ravens quarterback faked a handoff to running back Mark Ingram. The blitzing Miami Dolphins charged toward Ingram. That gave Jackson a moment to look downfield. In a flash, he zipped a pass to wide receiver Marquise Brown, who caught the ball in the middle of the field. A Miami defender dove toward Brown's waist, but he easily broke free from the attempted tackle. No one else came close to the receiver as he sprinted into the end zone for a 47-yard touchdown.

The Ravens were playing the Dolphins in Week 1 of the 2019 National Football League (NFL) season. The long touchdown put Baltimore ahead 14–0 midway through the first quarter.

Wide receiver Marquise Brown (15) made his NFL debut in 2019.

And the precise pass was one of many that Jackson would complete throughout the game.

FINDING A GEM

Since arriving in Baltimore in 1996, the Ravens had been a mostly successful team. Because of that, they didn't have a lot of top draft picks. Instead, the Ravens relied on smart selections later in the first round. This was perhaps never truer than in 2018.

Jackson had been one of the most explosive players in college football during his time at Louisville. As a sophomore in 2016, Jackson won the Heisman Trophy, which is awarded to the best player in college football. He followed that up with an excellent junior season. Few players could match Jackson's production in college. Yet NFL scouts didn't consider him the top quarterback in the 2018 draft class.

At Louisville, Jackson showcased an elite ability to run with the football. He could evade defenders with his speed, quickness, and agility. But some scouts worried about his passing accuracy. One former NFL general manager even suggested that Jackson should play wide receiver in the league.

Thirty-one players were picked ahead of Jackson in the 2018 draft. Four of them were quarterbacks. Even the Ravens passed on Jackson with the 25th pick. But when Jackson was still available at the final pick in the first round, the Ravens traded for the pick and selected the young quarterback.

The decision paid off early for Baltimore. After a 4–5 start to the 2018 season, the Ravens handed Jackson his first start in Week 11. His running ability provided Baltimore's offense the spark it needed. Jackson led the Ravens to a 6–1 run to end the season to secure the division title. However, his struggles to pass the ball stood out in his playoff debut, leading to a 23–17 loss to the Los Angeles Chargers.

Jackson was one of two Louisville players selected in the first round of the 2018 draft.

Jackson, *left*, ran for 695 yards in 2018.

HOT START

After seeing Jackson's passing struggles, some Baltimore fans wondered whether the Ravens had made a mistake in picking him. But the team showed confidence in its young quarterback and named him the starter for the 2019 season. Jackson proved why it was the right decision in Week 1 against the Dolphins by doing a lot more with his arm than his legs.

Baltimore jumped out to an early 7–0 lead in the first quarter. After the Dolphins threw an interception, the Ravens got the ball back on Miami's 47-yard line. On the next play, Jackson hit Brown for a touchdown. Then the Ravens forced the Dolphins to punt, giving Jackson the ball back at Baltimore's 10-yard line.

Jackson, *right*, celebrates with receiver Willie Snead after a touchdown in the 2019 game between the Ravens and the Miami Dolphins.

On third-and-three, Jackson dropped back to pass. His offensive line gave him a long time to stand in the pocket and scan the field. Jackson saw Brown streaking down the middle of the field and lofted the ball 45 yards. Brown caught it in stride and ran for an 83-yard touchdown. With 4:17 left in the first quarter, Baltimore already led 21–0.

Jackson kept the Baltimore offense rolling after that.

On the next drive, he delivered a perfect pass to wide receiver Willie Snead for a 33-yard score. Later in the second quarter, the Ravens were once again near the Dolphins' goal line. When Jackson dropped back to pass, a free Miami rusher ran straight toward him. That pressure didn't faze Jackson, though. He calmly backpedaled and lobbed a pass off his back foot that found wide receiver Miles Boykin for another touchdown.

Jackson capped off his day with a short pass for another score midway through the third quarter. After tossing five touchdown passes in seven starts during the 2018 season, Jackson started the 2019 campaign with five scoring passes to lead the Ravens to a 59–10 victory. The stellar performance was a sign of things to come for the rising star.

MORE THAN A RUNNER

Lamar Jackson's 324 passing yards and five touchdowns against the Dolphins were both career highs for one game. Jackson completed 17 of his 20 pass attempts and finished the game with a perfect passer rating of 158.3. During a post-game press conference, a reporter asked the quarterback whether he thought he proved that he could throw the ball effectively. Jackson jokingly answered, "Not bad for a running back."

Jackson finished the 2019 season with 3,127 passing yards.

NFL TEAMS MAP

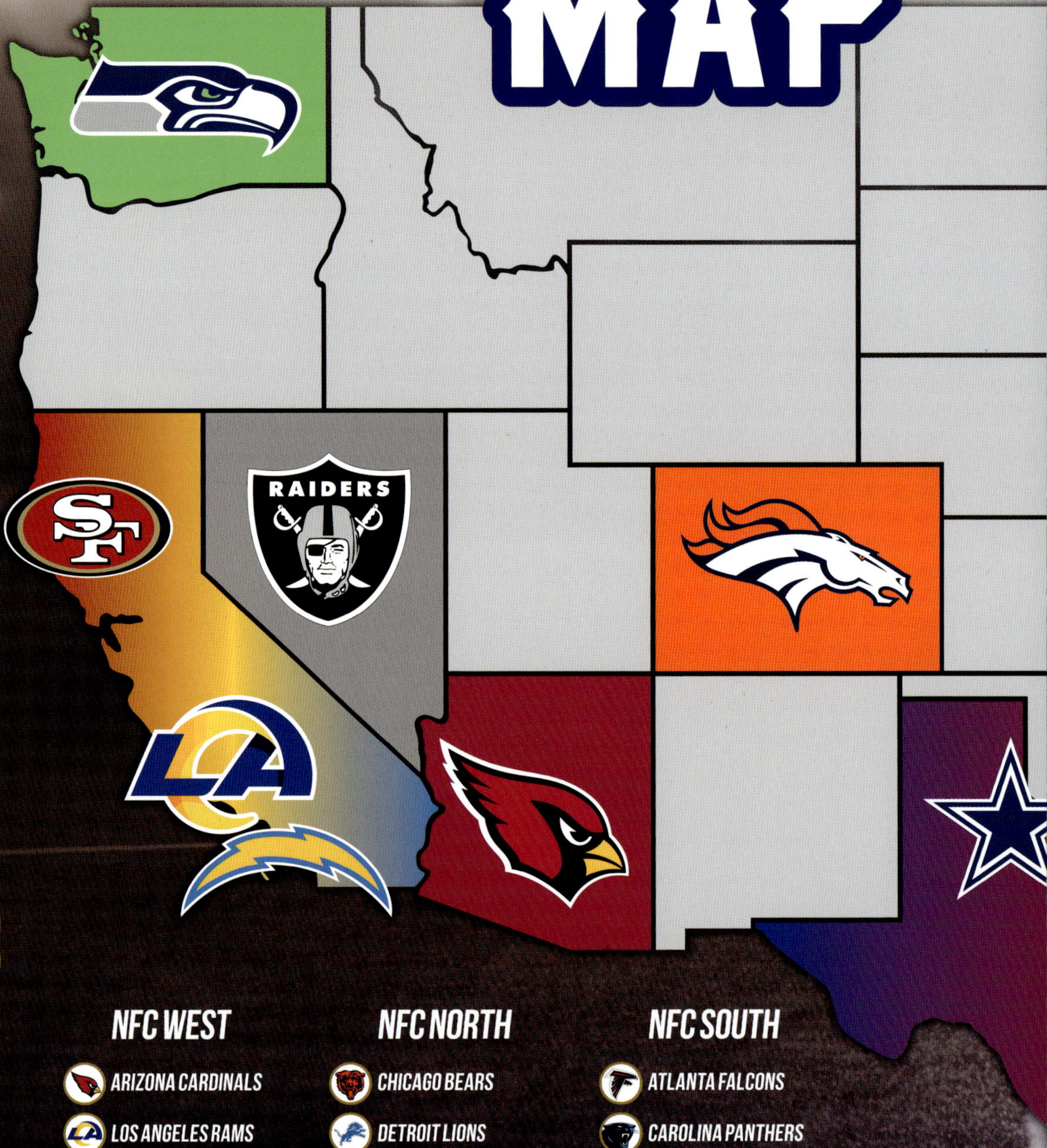

NFC EAST

NFC WEST

NFC NORTH

NFC SOUTH

AFC

AFC EAST

- BUFFALO BILLS
- MIAMI DOLPHINS
- NEW ENGLAND PATRIOTS
- NEW YORK JETS

AFC WEST

- DENVER BRONCOS
- KANSAS CITY CHIEFS
- LAS VEGAS RAIDERS
- LOS ANGELES CHARGERS

AFC NORTH

- BALTIMORE RAVENS
- CINCINNATI BENGALS
- CLEVELAND BROWNS
- PITTSBURGH STEELERS

AFC SOUTH

- HOUSTON TEXANS
- INDIANAPOLIS COLTS

- JACKSONVILLE JAGUARS
- TENNESSEE TITANS

Quarterback Johnny Unitas played for the Baltimore Colts from 1956 to 1972.

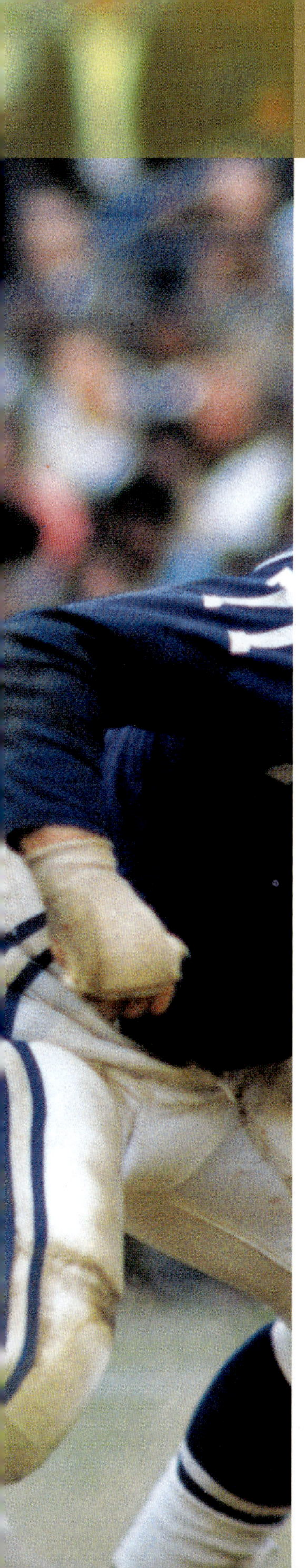

CHAPTER 2

BACK IN BALTIMORE

The city of Baltimore had plenty of experience with professional football before the Ravens showed up. From 1947 to 1950, a team called the Baltimore Colts played in several pro leagues. Then, in 1953, a different Baltimore Colts team played in its first NFL season. Through the play of legendary quarterback Johnny Unitas, the Colts won the NFL championship in 1958 and 1959. More than a decade later, Unitas helped the Colts win Super Bowl V following the 1970 season.

The Colts were one of the NFL's most stable franchises. Then in 1972, businessman Robert Irsay gained control of the team. For years after, he tried to get the city to pay for improvements to the existing stadium. When that didn't happen, Irsay decided to move the team. On March 28, 1984, moving trucks full of the team's equipment

A moving truck filled with the Colts' team equipment leaves Baltimore at night in March 1984.

left Baltimore in the middle of the night to move the franchise to Indianapolis. In an instant, Irsay left the city without an NFL team.

In the early 1990s, multiple groups tried to bring professional football back to Baltimore. The NFL planned to add two teams in 1995, and Baltimore appeared likely to get one. Instead, the league chose the cities of Charlotte and Jacksonville. Once that bid failed, Peter Angelos, the owner of the Baltimore Orioles Major League Baseball team, tried twice to move existing football teams to the city. But each time, the league shut him down. It seemed as if pro football in Baltimore would remain a thing of the past.

BROWNS ON THE MOVE

A new opportunity arose for Baltimore in 1995. The Cleveland Browns were close to going bankrupt. The team's owner, Art Modell, was losing money due to the city's outdated football stadium. So, Modell decided to move the Browns to Baltimore.

When teams move to a new city, they often keep the same team name. Even if they don't, they always keep the team's history. The NFL didn't want the history of the Browns out of Cleveland, though. The Browns had joined the NFL in 1950. By 1964, they had won four league championships. Cleveland was also a football-loving city. As a compromise, the league let Modell move the team, but it would have to go by a new name. Baltimore would be considered an expansion team, while the history of the Browns, including the logo and team colors, would stay in Cleveland. A new Cleveland Browns team started playing in the NFL in 1999.

Many Cleveland Browns fans were angered by Art Modell's decision to move the team to Baltimore.

Baltimore's executives eventually settled on three choices for a new nickname, which were the Americans, Marauders, and Ravens. More than 33,000 fans called in to vote on their favorite, and an overwhelming majority selected the Ravens. The name was inspired by the famous poem "The Raven" by Edgar Allan Poe, who lived in Baltimore for many years during the 1800s.

PERFECT DRAFT

The Ravens decided to keep the Browns' roster, but Modell brought in new people to run the team. Ted Marchibroda had coached the Baltimore Colts from 1975 to 1979. Modell hired Marchibroda to be the Ravens' first coach. Modell also hired former Browns' tight end Ozzie Newsome to be Baltimore's general manager.

It didn't take long for Newsome to have a big impact on the team. The Ravens had two picks in the first round of the 1996 NFL Draft. With the fourth pick, Newsome selected Jonathan Ogden. The powerful offensive lineman had a massive 6-foot-9-inch, 345-pound frame. Despite that size, Ogden had quick feet. Many offensive linemen block better on either running or passing plays. With his impressive blend of size and skill, Ogden excelled at both.

With the 26th pick, the Ravens drafted Ray Lewis out of the University of Miami. At 6-foot-1 and 240 pounds, Lewis was smaller than many NFL middle linebackers. However, he made up for it with an

POETIC MASCOTS

Most NFL teams have one mascot. But the Ravens decided to have three. At Baltimore's first home game in 1998, the team revealed its new mascots. Before the game, three ravens, named Edgar, Allan, and Poe, hatched out of three eggs on the field. They were named in honor of famous poet Edgar Allan Poe.

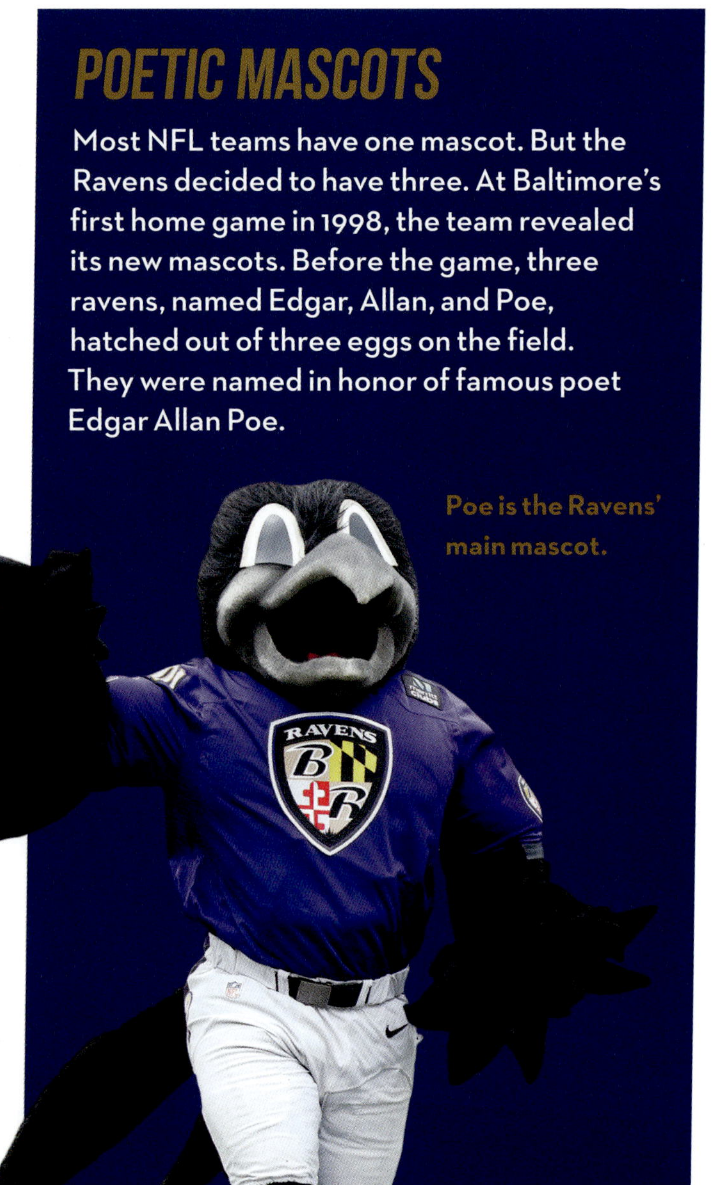

Poe is the Ravens' main mascot.

aggressive playing style and relentless effort. Lewis was also a natural leader capable of firing up his teammates with rousing pregame speeches. "Ray is the greatest leader in team sports history," said future Ravens tight end Shannon Sharpe. "No one is even close."

"RAY IS THE GREATEST LEADER IN TEAM SPORTS HISTORY. NO ONE IS EVEN CLOSE."

—SHANNON SHARPE

The Ravens played their first NFL game on September 1, 1996. More than 64,000 fans packed into Memorial Stadium, which is where the Baltimore Colts used to play. In his NFL debut, Lewis thrilled the crowd with an interception. The Ravens defeated the Oakland Raiders 19–14 to pick up their first win.

Offensive lineman Jonathan Ogden, *right*, poses with NFL commissioner Paul Tagliabue during the 1996 draft.

Both Ogden and Lewis made an immediate impact as rookies. Lewis led the Ravens in tackles with 110. Meanwhile, Ogden helped the Ravens offense record the third-most yards in the league.

However, the Ravens struggled as a team, finishing their first season 4–12.

Quarterback Vinny Testaverde (12) celebrates with Ravens fans after the team's first NFL touchdown.

FINDING AN IDENTITY

After posting a 6–9–1 record in 1997, the Ravens had a new home for the 1998 season. Playing at Ravens Stadium didn't change the fortune of the team much, though. Baltimore once again won six games, but the season did feature one major highlight for Ravens fans.

In Week 13, the Indianapolis Colts traveled to Baltimore for the first time since the team left in 1984. More than 68,000 fans were in attendance, and they were desperate to beat the team that left their city. The Colts jumped out to a 24–10 lead, and they continued to lead 31–21 at the start of the fourth quarter. But the Ravens scored two touchdowns in less than two minutes to take their first lead, and then defensive back Ralph Staten intercepted Colts quarterback Peyton Manning late in the fourth to secure the 38–31 comeback win.

After the 1998 season, the Ravens fired Marchibroda.

Linebacker Ray Lewis recorded 2,059 tackles during his career.

Brian Billick accumulated an 80–64 record during his nine years as the Ravens' head coach.

Modell replaced him with head coach Brian Billick, who had been the offensive coordinator for a Minnesota Vikings team that posted a record 556 points in 1998. The Ravens hoped that Billick could bring a similarly explosive offense to Baltimore.

Billick ended up leading Baltimore to its best record yet in 1999. But it wasn't due to the offense lighting up the scoreboard. By that season, Lewis had established himself as one of the best defensive players in the NFL. He recorded a league-high 165 tackles. Meanwhile, second-year safety Rod Woodson led the NFL with seven interceptions.

Both Lewis and Woodson made the Pro Bowl that year after anchoring one of the best defenses in the NFL. The duo helped the Ravens go 8–8 to avoid a losing season. And Baltimore's defense would only get better after that.

Safety Rod Woodson returned 12 interceptions for touchdowns during his career, which is an NFL record.

The Ravens recorded four shutout wins during the 2000 season.

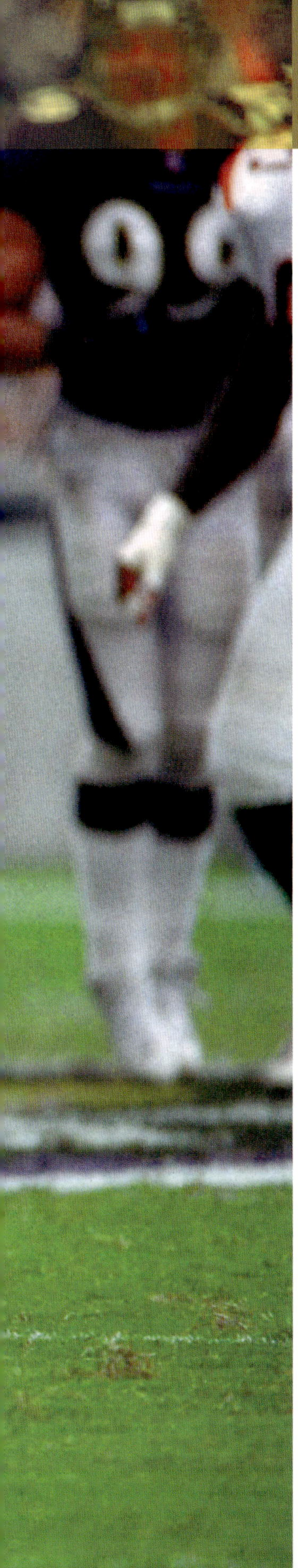

CHAPTER 3

DEFENSE WINS CHAMPIONSHIPS

THE RAVENS BEGAN THE 2000 SEASON WITH A TRIP TO PITTSBURGH to face off against the division rival Steelers. Ray Lewis led a dominant display as the Baltimore defense shut out the Steelers 16–0 to start the season with a win. The performance served as a sign of things to come.

The Ravens had some offensive standouts in 2000. Running back Jamal Lewis had been the fifth overall pick in that year's draft. As a rookie, he racked up 1,364 rushing yards. In Week 2, tight end Shannon Sharpe scored a touchdown with 41 seconds left to lift the Ravens to a 39–36 win against the Jacksonville Jaguars. The veteran went on to lead the team in receiving yards.

However, the Ravens' overwhelming strength that season was their defense. Ray Lewis and Rod Woodson were both back to their best.

During the 2000 season, the Ravens' defense allowed a league-low 60.6 rushing yards per game.

They helped the team record three shutouts in its first five games. Baltimore's defense had become such a force that it made up for its faltering offense. In Weeks 5 and 6, the Ravens won games in which they didn't score a single touchdown. But the defense allowed only 10.3 points per game all season. The Ravens also allowed just 165 total points, the fewest ever given up by any team in a 16-game NFL season.

Running back Jamal Lewis ran for more than 100 yards in five games during the 2000 season.

GETTING THE JOB DONE

Baltimore finished the 2000 season with a 12–4 record to clinch its first playoff berth. The Ravens started their run in the postseason with a home game against the Denver Broncos. Everything came together for Baltimore as Jamal Lewis scored two touchdowns, and Sharpe added a 58-yard score. On defense, Ray Lewis recorded an interception as the Ravens gave up only one field goal to secure a 21–3 victory.

The Ravens' defense and special teams stepped up again against the Tennessee Titans in the divisional round. With the game tied 10–10 early in the fourth quarter, Baltimore blocked a Tennessee field-goal attempt. Ravens defensive back Anthony Mitchell scooped up the ball and raced 90 yards for a touchdown. With 6:41 to go, Ray Lewis intercepted a pass that tipped off the hands of Titans star running back Eddie George. Lewis dashed 50 yards for a touchdown to seal Baltimore's 24–10 win.

Defensive back Anthony Mitchell celebrates after returning a blocked field goal 90 yards for a touchdown against the Tennessee Titans.

The Ravens kept rolling in the American Football Conference (AFC) title game against the Oakland Raiders. Early in the second quarter, Sharpe caught a pass over the middle of the field and took it 96 yards for a touchdown. Baltimore's defense then recorded

Tight end Shannon Sharpe, *in white*, scored the only touchdown in the divisional matchup between the Ravens and Oakland Raiders after the 2000 season.

four interceptions and allowed just one field goal in a 16–3 win. The victory booked the Ravens a trip to Super Bowl XXXV.

In a season full of stellar defensive performances from the Ravens, the Super Bowl may have been the best of all. The Ravens picked off New York Giants quarterback Kerry Collins four times. That included a 49-yard pick six by Duane Starks in the third quarter to put the Ravens up 17–0. The only points the Giants scored came on a kickoff return for a touchdown in the third quarter. But right

Ray Lewis led the Ravens' defense in Super Bowl XXXV in January 2001.

after the Giants scored, Baltimore's Jermaine Lewis returned the next kick for a touchdown. The defense shut the door after that to help the Ravens win 34–7 and claim their first Super Bowl title.

HARD TO REPEAT

The Ravens' quest to defend their Super Bowl title got off to a bad start. During a practice in August 2001, Jamal Lewis suffered a season-ending knee injury. With the team's best offensive player out, the Baltimore defense was forced to step up again.

While the defense didn't match its level from the 2000 season, it still featured the elite duo of Woodson and Ray Lewis. They helped the Ravens enter the final week of the season with a 9–6 record.

Baltimore hosted the Minnesota Vikings knowing a win would secure a playoff spot. After giving up a field goal in the first quarter, the Ravens' defense didn't allow another point. Linebacker Jamie Sharper also recovered a fumble for a touchdown in a 19–3 victory.

The Ravens traveled to Miami for the wild-card round to play the Dolphins. Just as they had a week prior, the Ravens fell behind 3–0. And once again, the defense did not allow another point. Baltimore won 20–3 to set up a meeting with the Steelers in Pittsburgh. However, the lack of offense finally sank the Ravens, as the only touchdown they scored came off a punt return. The Steelers won 27–10 to end Baltimore's season.

THE RICH GET RICHER

In the 2002 NFL Draft, the Ravens selected another great defensive player out of the University of Miami in Ed Reed. The safety seemed to always have his eyes on the quarterback. If an opposing passer threw the ball in Reed's direction, it often ended up in his hands. Reed led the Ravens with five interceptions as a rookie.

HISTORIC SEASON

Few defensive players have had a more successful season than Ray Lewis did in 2000. The linebacker won the Defensive Player of the Year Award for his role in leading a record-breaking defense. He then won the Super Bowl XXXV Most Valuable Player (MVP) Award after recording five tackles and breaking up four passes in the win over the New York Giants. Lewis became just the seventh defensive player to earn MVP honors in Super Bowl history. And he was only the second player to be named both the Defensive Player of the Year and Super Bowl MVP in the same season.

The Ravens continued to build up their strong defense in the 2003 draft. With the 10th pick that year, Baltimore selected

Terrell Suggs. The outside linebacker combined brute strength with explosive quickness to torment opposing quarterbacks. Suggs recorded 12 sacks in 2003 to earn the Defensive Rookie of the Year Award. Meanwhile, Ray Lewis intercepted a career-high six passes that season and won his second Defensive Player of the Year Award.

While the Ravens' defense featured tons of talent, no Baltimore player had a better 2003 season than Jamal Lewis. The running back returned from his knee injury looking just as good as he did

The Ravens' defense gave up just 151 total yards in the team's playoff win against the Miami Dolphins in January 2002.

in 2000. In Week 2 against the Cleveland Browns, Jamal Lewis took his first carry of the game for an 82-yard touchdown. He finished the game with an NFL-record 295 rushing yards. Later in the year, he torched the Browns again, this time rushing for 205 yards. Lewis ended the year with 2,066 rushing yards, making him only the fifth player in NFL history to rush for more than 2,000 yards in a season.

Many football fans consider Ed Reed one of the best safeties of all time.

Even with elite talent on offense and defense, the Ravens stumbled in the playoffs. The Titans traveled to Baltimore and beat the Ravens 20–17 in the wild-card round. The Ravens looked to turn things around the following season.

A BALTIMORE TRADITION

After the Super Bowl run in 2000, the Ravens searched for a quarterback to stabilize their offense. Six quarterbacks started a game for Baltimore between 2001 and 2005. But none of them could lift the offense. So, in 2006, the Ravens traded for a proven veteran quarterback. Steve McNair had led the Titans to a Super Bowl appearance after the 1999 season and had won co-Most Valuable Player (MVP) honors in 2003. He had also knocked the Ravens out of the playoffs that season. However, after joining Baltimore, McNair helped elevate the Ravens' offense.

While the offense vastly improved, the defense continued to be the strength of the team. Ray Lewis, Reed, and Suggs led the Ravens to a team-record 13 wins in the regular season. Baltimore earned a bye in the first round of the playoffs and hosted the Indianapolis Colts in the divisional round.

More than 70,000 Baltimore fans packed

Jamal Lewis (31) ran for more than 100 yards in 12 games during the 2003 season. He had more than 200 rushing yards in two of those games.

Terrell Suggs, *right*, and Ray Lewis, *left*, each won the Defensive Player of the Year Award during their careers with the Ravens.

Billick, *left*, talks to quarterback Kyle Boller during the 2007 game between the Ravens and Cleveland Browns.

their home stadium desperate to beat the Colts. As usual, the defense stepped up under pressure. Facing future Hall of Fame quarterback Peyton Manning, the Ravens didn't allow a touchdown. Reed picked off Manning twice. But the offense couldn't get anything going. The Ravens turned the ball over four times en route to a 15–6 loss.

Everything fell apart for the Ravens during the 2007 season. That year, three Baltimore quarterbacks combined to throw a total of 13 touchdowns and 14 interceptions. The low point of the season came in Week 15 when the Ravens lost in overtime to the previously winless Miami Dolphins. Once the season ended, Baltimore fired Brian Billick after nine seasons as head coach.

Ravens owner Steve Bisciotti, *left*, introduces John Harbaugh, *right*, as the team's new head coach.

CHAPTER 4

QUICK TURNAROUND

HEADING INTO THE 2008 SEASON, THE RAVENS NEEDED A NEW HEAD coach. The team decided to hire John Harbaugh, a longtime assistant coach at the college and pro levels. Most NFL teams hire coaches with previous head coaching experience, or someone who had been an offensive or defensive coordinator. Harbaugh had never overseen a defense or offense. He arrived in Baltimore after coaching the Philadelphia Eagles' special teams and secondary. Some analysts questioned the hire. But the Ravens were convinced that Harbaugh was the right man for the job.

The Ravens made another significant addition during the 2008 offseason. In that year's draft, the team selected quarterback Joe Flacco in the first round. As with the Harbaugh hire, football analysts questioned the Flacco pick.

Flacco couldn't win the starting job at the University of Pittsburgh. He ended up transferring to Delaware, a smaller school that played at a less competitive level. Flacco thrived at Delaware. However, some scouts thought he wouldn't be able to handle the tougher competition in the NFL.

Baltimore's decision to go with Harbaugh and Flacco paid off. While Flacco didn't put up monster stats during his rookie season, he led an effective offense while not making a ton of mistakes.

Quarterback Joe Flacco (5) threw for 2,971 yards and 14 touchdowns during his rookie season with Baltimore.

Meanwhile, Ray Lewis, Terrell Suggs, and Ed Reed kept the Baltimore defense as one of the league's best.

When the playoffs rolled around, the defense made Flacco's job a lot easier. In the wild-card round, the Ravens traveled to Miami to play the Dolphins. Late in the first half, Reed picked off a deep pass and returned it 64 yards for the game's first touchdown. On offense, the Ravens relied on their running game. Flacco even scored a rushing touchdown himself to secure a 27–9 win.

Ed Reed, *center*, returns an interception against the Dolphins during a playoff game in January 2009.

In the divisional round, the Ravens took on the Tennessee Titans, the top seed in the conference. Neither team could produce much offense. With 4:17 left and the game tied 10–10, the Ravens started a drive on their own 24-yard line. On third-and-two, Flacco completed a 23-yard pass to get the Ravens past midfield. The rookie then led the offense into field-goal range. With 53 seconds left, kicker Matt Stover drilled a 43-yard field goal to put Baltimore up 13–10. The defense then stopped the Titans to secure the win and send the Ravens to the AFC Championship Game.

Flacco's inexperience finally caught up with him in the AFC title game. Against the rival Pittsburgh Steelers, the rookie threw three interceptions. That included a pick six that sealed Baltimore's defeat.

While the season came to a disappointing end, the Ravens knew they had a coach and a quarterback they could win with.

COMING UP SHORT

Harbaugh and Flacco built off the success of the 2008 season. The Ravens made the playoffs again in 2009. They steamrolled the New England Patriots in the wild-card round thanks to 159 rushing yards from running back Ray Rice. The Baltimore defense also created four turnovers during the game. However, the Ravens lost to the Indianapolis Colts a week later.

Terrell Suggs, *front right*, recorded four sacks during the playoffs after the 2008 season.

The next year, Baltimore had a 12–4 record but finished just behind the Steelers in the AFC North. After a blowout victory over the Kansas City Chiefs in the wild-card round, the Ravens traveled to Pittsburgh to face their biggest rival. The teams were back and forth throughout the physical game. But the Steelers scored a touchdown with 1:33 left to seal a 31–24 win.

The Ravens made up for the tough loss by beating the Steelers twice in the 2011 regular season. They also won their division. After defeating the Houston Texans in the divisional round, the Ravens headed to New England to play the Patriots in the AFC Championship Game. The Patriots took a 23–20 lead early in the fourth quarter. With 1:44 left, the Ravens started a drive on their own 21-yard line. Flacco comfortably guided the offense down the field. With less than 30 seconds remaining, Flacco threaded a perfect pass to wide receiver Lee Evans in the end zone. But a New England defender knocked the ball away from Evans. The Ravens had to go for a 32-yard field goal to tie the game. However, kicker Billy Cundiff booted the ball wide left of the goalpost.

"WE HAVE TO COME BACK AND GO TO WORK TO MAKE SURE WE FINISH IT NEXT TIME."

—RAY LEWIS

In the locker room after the game, Ray Lewis addressed the entire team. He told his teammates that the loss didn't come down to one play. He said, "We have to come back and go to work to make sure we finish it next time."

COMING BACK STRONGER

Lewis's words resonated with the team. During the 2012 season, the Ravens jumped out to a 9–2 record. However, the team faded

Kicker Billy Cundiff (7) misses a field goal in the AFC title game against the New England Patriots in January 2012.

down the stretch. Lewis hadn't played since Week 6 after tearing his triceps early in the season. The Ravens lost four of their final five regular-season games. Even with those losses, they still finished atop their division and hosted the Colts in the playoffs.

Lewis recovered from his injury and prepared to return for a playoff run. Days before facing the Colts, Lewis announced that he was retiring after the season. Throughout most of his career, Lewis would do a signature dance while being introduced during home games. When he did it before facing the Colts in the playoffs, the home crowd erupted. The Baltimore defense fed off the energy of the crowd by not allowing a touchdown in a comfortable 24–9 win.

Running back Ray Rice recorded 37 rushing touchdowns during his six seasons with the Ravens.

In the divisional round, the Ravens played on the road against the Denver Broncos, the top team in the conference. Despite giving up two special teams touchdowns, the Ravens were able to respond. Flacco delivered a masterful performance, throwing 59-yard and 32-yard touchdown passes in the first half to wide receiver Torrey Smith. The Ravens still needed more out of Flacco, though. Down 35–28 with 1:09 left, the Ravens got the ball to their own 23-yard line. After running for 7 yards, Flacco got his team lined up for a third-and-three with the clock winding down.

Ray Lewis, *right*, had 13 tackles against the Indianapolis Colts in a playoff game after the 2012 season.

On the next play, Flacco unleashed a 50-yard pass down the field. With a Broncos defender falling over in coverage, the ball fell right into the hands of wide receiver Jacoby Jones for a 70-yard touchdown. The Ravens eventually won 38–35 in double overtime thanks to a game-winning 47-yard field goal by kicker Justin Tucker.

Baltimore got revenge against the Patriots the following week to book a trip to Super Bowl XLVII. Waiting for the Ravens were the San Francisco 49ers, who were coached by Jim Harbaugh, John's brother. In a game dubbed "the Harbaugh Bowl," the Ravens came out of the gate flying. Jones caught a 56-yard touchdown pass from Flacco near the end of the first half to put Baltimore up 21–3. Then to start the second half, Jones returned the kickoff 108 yards for a score to extend the lead to 28–6.

BITTERSWEET MOMENT

In 2011, the Ravens defeated the San Francisco 49ers in a regular-season game. John and Jim Harbaugh's parents, Jack and Jackie, went to congratulate John on the victory. When they walked in the locker room and saw how happy John was, they knew they weren't needed there. Jim, on the other hand, was sitting alone after the game with his head in his hands. After the brothers met in the next season's Super Bowl, Jack and Jackie knew they needed to console the son who lost more than they needed to celebrate with the son who won.

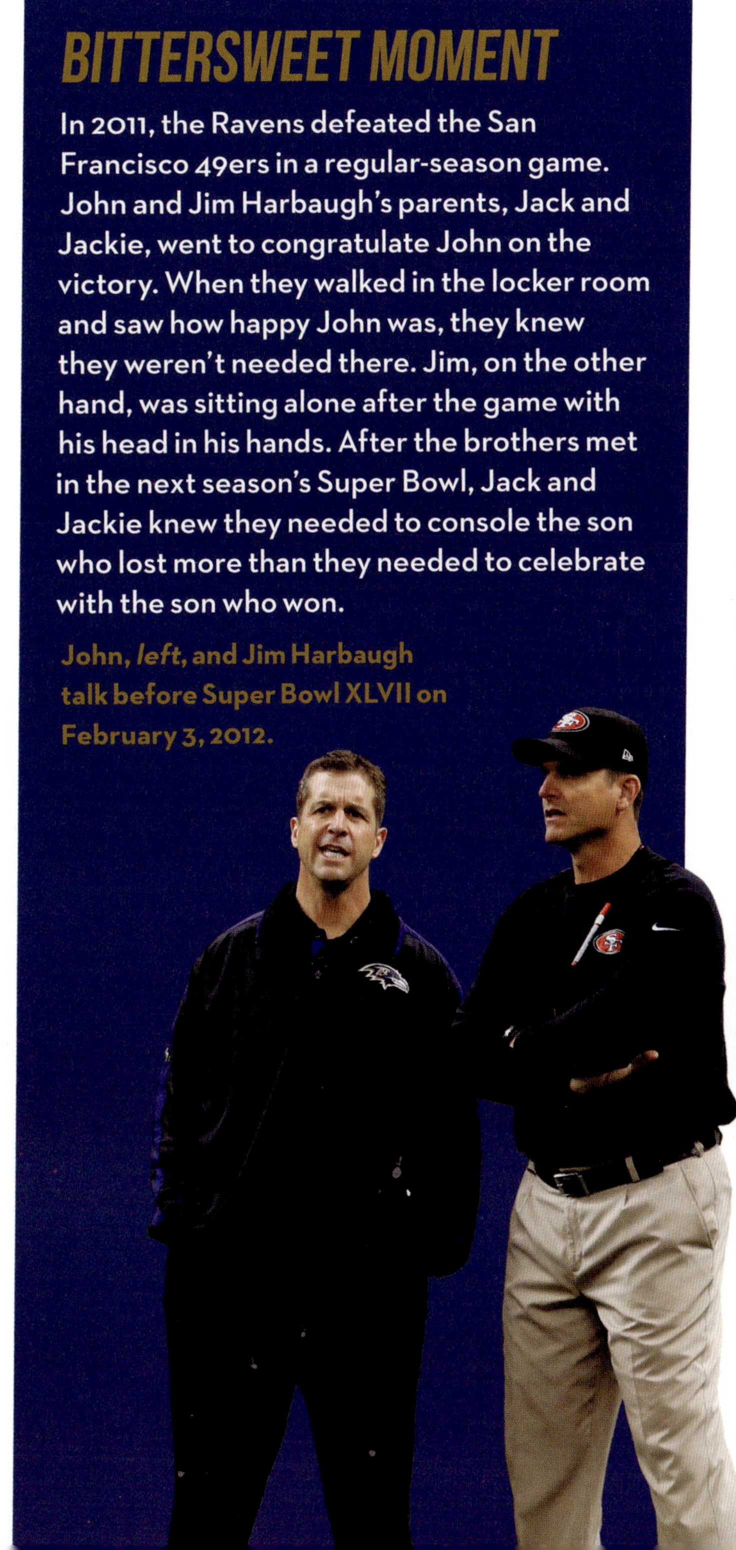

John, *left*, and Jim Harbaugh talk before Super Bowl XLVII on February 3, 2012.

Wide receiver Jacoby Jones became the ninth player to return a kickoff for a touchdown in Super Bowl history.

Ray Lewis hoists the Vince Lombardi Trophy after the Ravens won Super Bowl XLVII.

It seemed as if the Ravens would easily win. However, with 13:22 left in the third quarter, some of the lights in the stadium went out. The power outage led to a 34-minute delay in the game. Once the lights turned back on, the 49ers looked like a new team. They scored 17 consecutive points to get back in the game heading into the fourth quarter.

With the Ravens up 34–29, the 49ers got the ball back with 4:19 to go. San Francisco quarterback Colin Kaepernick drove his offense down to the Baltimore 5-yard line. But the Ravens' defense forced three straight incomplete passes to keep the 49ers out of the end zone. The Ravens held on to win 34–31, giving John Harbaugh bragging rights over his brother. The win also sent Ray Lewis into retirement with his second Super Bowl ring.

In Super Bowl XLVII, Joe Flacco threw for 287 yards and three touchdowns.

CHAPTER 5

COMING BACK TO EARTH

JOE FLACCO PLAYED AT AN ELITE LEVEL DURING THE PLAYOFFS AFTER the 2012 season. In four games, he threw 11 touchdowns. He capped it off with an MVP performance in the Super Bowl. The Ravens rewarded Flacco with a massive six-year contract extension before the 2013 season.

Flacco couldn't find the same form during the 2013 season, though. He threw more interceptions than touchdowns, and he was sacked a career-high 48 times. The Ravens finished with an 8–8 record and missed the playoffs for the first time in Flacco's career.

The Ravens faced more trouble during the offseason. In March 2014, star running back Ray Rice was arrested on an assault charge for an incident involving his girlfriend. The NFL initially suspended him for two games, until a video of the incident was released that September. After seeing the video, the Ravens released Rice, and he never played in the NFL again.

Flacco bounced back in 2014 to help the Ravens return to the playoffs. The veteran quarterback tossed a pair of touchdown passes to help Baltimore beat the Pittsburgh Steelers 30–17 in the wild-card round. The next week, Baltimore fell to the New England Patriots. Despite the loss, the Ravens looked as though they were headed back in the right direction with Flacco leading the way.

MAKING A CHANGE

The momentum from the 2014 season didn't last long. Over the next three years, the Ravens never won more than nine games, and they missed the playoffs each time. With every passing season, Flacco looked less and less like the quarterback that had lifted

Receiver Torrey Smith, *right*, attempts to make a catch in a playoff game against the Pittsburgh Steelers in January 2015.

Flacco (5) recorded 3,986 passing yards during the 2014 season.

Lamar Jackson (8) evades multiple Cincinnati Bengals defenders during a 2019 game.

Baltimore to a Super Bowl title. So, the team selected quarterback Lamar Jackson in the first round of the 2018 draft. After Flacco's struggles continued into the 2018 season, Jackson took over. He led the Ravens back to the playoffs. After the season, the Ravens traded Flacco to the Denver Broncos and officially handed the team's offense over to Jackson.

Jackson quickly showed that the Ravens had made the right decision. After hearing doubts all offseason about his throwing ability, Jackson dished out five touchdown passes in a Week 1 blowout win against the Miami Dolphins. He continued that form throughout 2019. Jackson threw for three or more touchdown passes in eight games that year.

While Jackson showed off his arm more in 2019, that didn't stop him from running the ball. His speed and elusiveness were on full display in a Week 10 game against the Cincinnati Bengals. Midway through the third quarter, Jackson faked a handoff and ran to the left. After sprinting past two defenders, he juked by another. Then, with two defenders zeroing in on him, Jackson spun to his right, leaving them both in the dust. He then ran all the way into the end zone for a 47-yard score.

Electric plays like that became a weekly occurrence for Jackson. He finished with 1,206 rushing yards. No quarterback had ever run for that many yards in a season. Jackson also led the NFL with 36 passing touchdowns. His stellar play on the ground and through the air earned him the league's MVP Award.

Jackson led Baltimore to a 14–2 record and a division title in 2019. The Ravens entered the playoffs looking like Super Bowl favorites. However, they struggled at home in the divisional round against the Tennessee Titans. On Baltimore's first drive, tight end Mark Andrews dropped a high throw from Jackson. The ball

Tight end Mark Andrews bobbles a pass against the Tennessee Titans in the playoffs in January 2020.

tipped off Andrews's hands directly to a Titans defender for an easy interception. On Baltimore's next offensive drive, Jackson turned the ball over after he couldn't find a running lane on a fourth-and-one play.

The Ravens had the highest-scoring offense in the league in 2019. Suddenly, that explosive offense had disappeared when it mattered most. Jackson finished the game with two interceptions and a fumble. The Titans also stopped the Ravens short on two

Jackson (8) started all but one game during the 2019 regular season.

fourth-down plays. Tennessee capitalized on those stops and cruised to a 28–12 upset to end Baltimore's season.

HISTORY REPEATS ITSELF

Jackson didn't let the disappointing end of the 2019 season roll into 2020. He continued to frustrate opposing defenses with both his arm and his legs. Jackson led the Ravens back to the playoffs, where they once again met the Titans. Only this time, the Ravens had to travel to Tennessee.

The Titans took an early 7–0 lead. When the Ravens got the ball back, Jackson severely underthrew a receiver downfield. The ball fell right into the hands of a Tennessee defensive back. Seven plays later, the Titans kicked a field goal to lead 10–0.

A RECORD KICK

In Week 3 of the 2021 season, the Ravens traveled to Detroit to play the Lions. The Ravens trailed the Lions 17–16 with three seconds left in the game. Baltimore had the ball at the Detroit 49-yard line. Ravens kicker Justin Tucker came on to attempt a 66-yard game-winning field goal. Tucker's kick bounced off the crossbar, went straight up, and dropped down just behind the bar. The kick was the longest in NFL history, beating the old record by 2 yards.

Kicker Justin Tucker (9) attempts a 66-yard field goal.

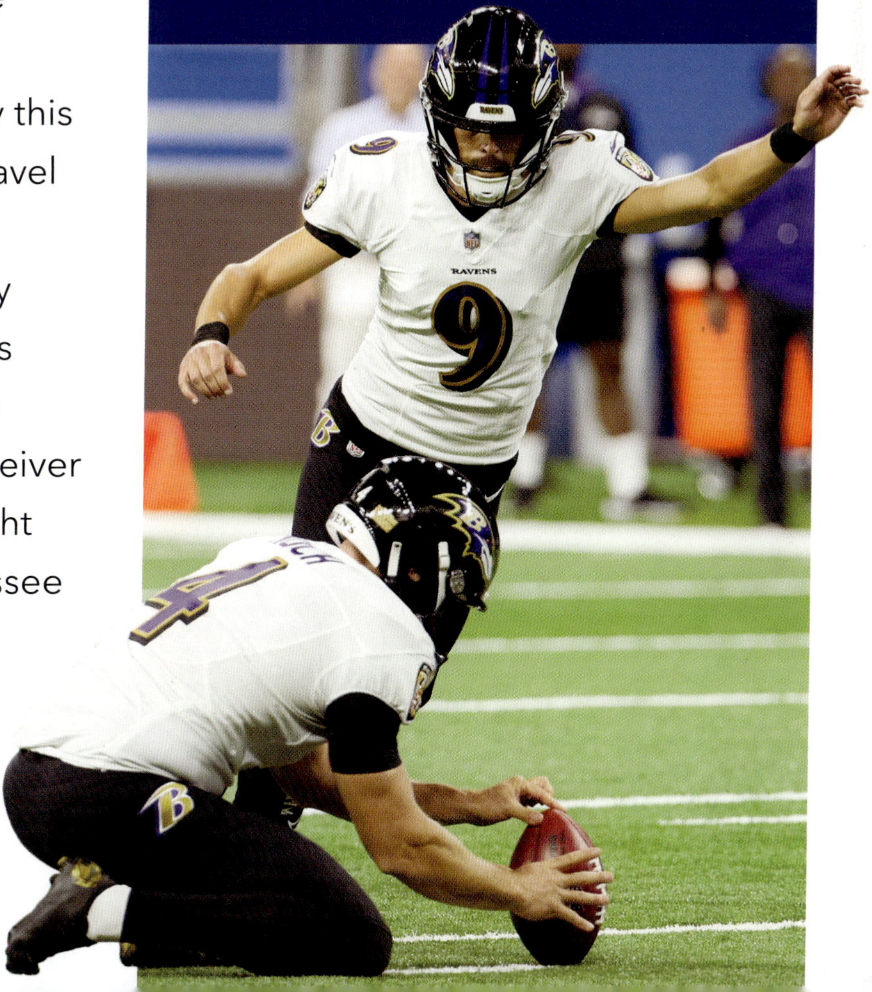

Jackson had 1,005 rushing yards and 2,757 passing yards during the 2020 season.

The mistakes didn't pile up for Jackson this time around, though. Late in the second quarter, he couldn't find any open receivers on a pass play. So, he tucked the ball and burst through a collapsing pocket. Jackson ran past four defenders before diving into the end zone for a 48-yard score to tie the game 10–10.

On Baltimore's first possession in the second half, Jackson carved up the Tennessee defense with his arm and legs. Ravens running back J. K. Dobbins closed out the drive with a 4-yard touchdown. Baltimore's defense finished the job from there, allowing the Titans only a field goal in the fourth quarter. The Ravens won 20–13, giving Jackson his first playoff win.

The Ravens had every chance to win in Buffalo when they faced the Bills in the 2020 divisional round. The Baltimore defense held superstar quarterback Josh Allen in check for most of the game. Down by seven late in the third quarter, the Ravens were driving for a tying score. On a third-and-goal play from Buffalo's 9-yard line, Jackson threw into tight traffic in the middle of the end zone. Bills defensive back Taron Johnson picked off the pass and returned it 101 yards for a touchdown. That play helped seal a 17–3 loss for the Ravens.

Running back J. K. Dobbins, *right*, had nine rushing touchdowns during his rookie season in 2020.

By age 22, Jackson had won an MVP Award and established himself as one of the league's top quarterbacks. But many fans began doubting his ability to lead the Ravens to a Super Bowl win. Those doubts continued to increase when Jackson suffered season-ending injuries in 2021 and 2022, forcing him to miss 10 games across both seasons. Even the Ravens didn't show complete confidence in Jackson. After the 2022 season, Baltimore took its time offering the quarterback a new deal. Other teams had a chance to make an offer to Jackson that the Ravens could match. But when no teams were willing to do that, Baltimore signed Jackson to a new five-year contract that made him the highest paid player in the league.

PROVIDING VALUE

With a hectic offseason behind him, Jackson showed why he was worth such a large contract. After a 3–2 start to the 2023 season, the Ravens won nine of their next 10 games. Then they played the Miami Dolphins in Week 17 with a chance to clinch the top record in their conference and secure a first-round bye in the playoffs. Jackson put together his best performance of the season, slinging five touchdowns to crush the Dolphins 56–19. That display helped Jackson secure his second MVP Award.

The Ravens took care of business in the divisional round to set up a conference-championship matchup against the defending Super Bowl champion Kansas City Chiefs. After the Chiefs took a

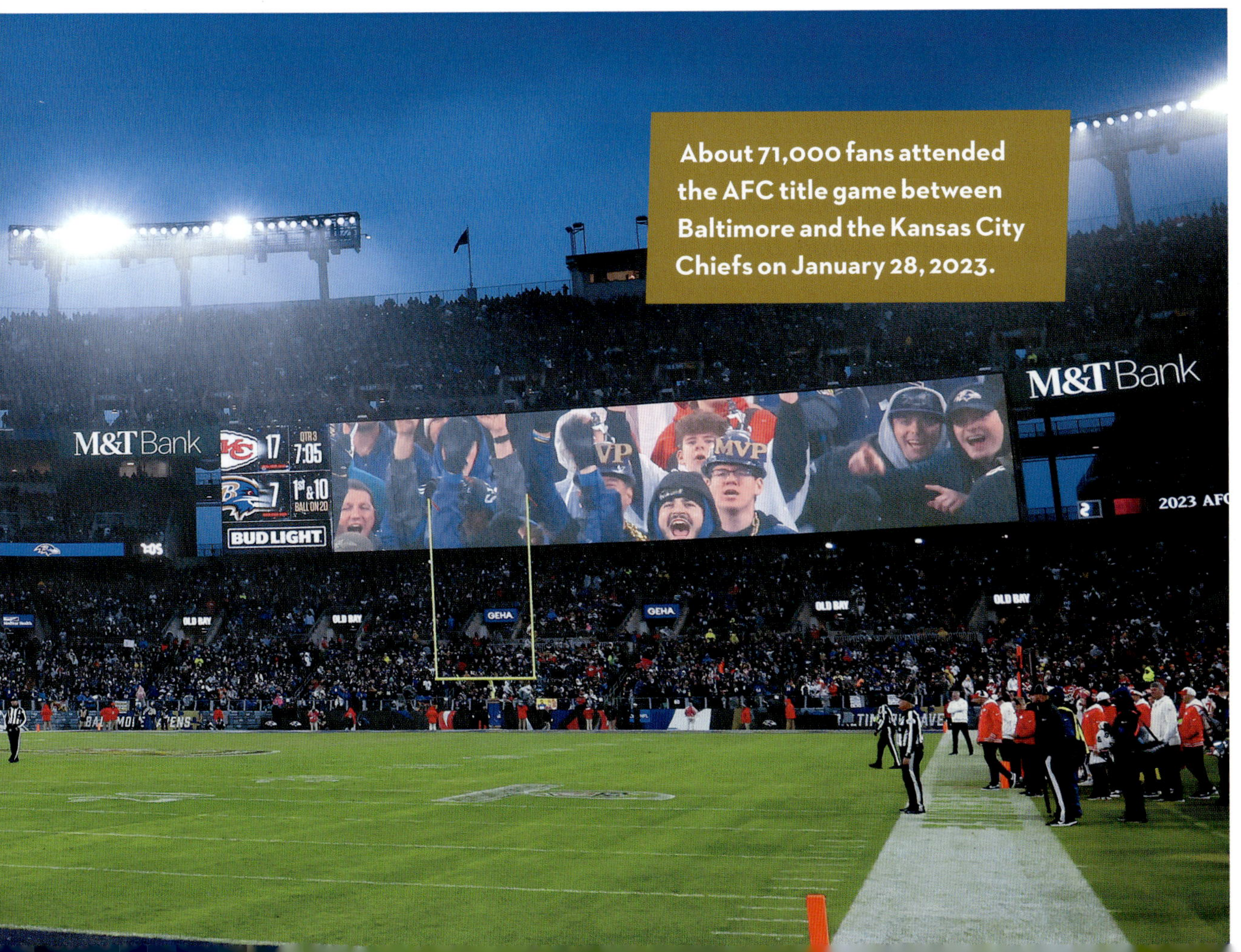

About 71,000 fans attended the AFC title game between Baltimore and the Kansas City Chiefs on January 28, 2023.

RAVENS TROPHY CASE

SUPER BOWL CHAMPIONSHIPS: 2

Super Bowl XXXV – January 28, 2001
Super Bowl XLVII – February 3, 2013

CONFERENCE CHAMPIONSHIPS: 2

2000, 2012

DIVISION TITLES: 8

AFC North: 2003, 2006, 2011, 2012, 2018, 2019, 2023, 2024

All stats are through the 2024 season.

XXXV

XLVII

quick 7–0 lead, Jackson responded with some magic. From Kansas City's 30-yard line, Jackson dropped back to pass. A Chiefs defender got to him in a hurry, but Jackson ducked away from the tackle, then moved back in the pocket to buy himself some time. That scramble allowed wide receiver Zay Flowers to get open downfield. Jackson hit Flowers in stride for a 30-yard touchdown.

The Chiefs answered and had a 17–7 lead going into halftime. Late in the third quarter, Jackson hit Flowers for a 54-yard gain to give the Ravens some life. Four plays later, Flowers caught a pass in the middle of the field, then dived toward the goal line. However, before he got into the end zone, he fumbled the ball away to the Chiefs to kill Baltimore's momentum. The Ravens never found the end zone again in a 17–10 loss.

Running back Derrick Henry rushed for a league-leading 16 touchdowns during the 2024 season.

Baltimore added superstar running back Derrick Henry before the 2024 season. After recording more than 2,000 total yards in the regular season, Henry ran for 186 in the Ravens' 28–14 wild-card round win over the Steelers. But the team came up short in the divisional round, falling to the Bills 27–25. Even though the Ravens suffered another heartbreaking playoff loss, fans remained hopeful that Jackson could bring the city another Super Bowl title.

TIMELINE

1996
The Baltimore Ravens play their first NFL game and defeat the Oakland Raiders 19–14.

The Indianapolis Colts travel to Baltimore for the first time since leaving the city. The Ravens win 38–31.
1998

The Ravens win Super Bowl XXXV on January 28.
2001

2003
Jamal Lewis runs for 2,066 yards, making him the fifth running back with 2,000 yards in a season.

2006
The Ravens win a then franchise-record 13 games but lose to the Colts in the playoffs.

Baltimore hires John Harbaugh as the team's head coach and selects Joe Flacco in the first round of the draft.
2008

Kicker Billy Cundiff misses a game-tying 32-yard field-goal attempt in the AFC title game on January 22 to end Baltimore's season.
2012

2013
In Ray Lewis's last season, the Ravens win Super Bowl XLVII on February 3.

2018
The Ravens select Lamar Jackson in the 2018 NFL Draft.

Jackson becomes the starter and is the first Ravens player to win the NFL's MVP Award.
2019

2021
The Ravens defeat the Tennessee Titans in the wild-card round on January 10, earning Jackson his first playoff win.

Jackson wins his second MVP Award and leads the Ravens to the AFC title game for the first time since 2012.
2023

GLOSSARY

bankrupt–unable to pay debts.

blitz–when a linebacker or defensive back attacks the line of scrimmage to stop a run or sack the quarterback.

conference–a subset of teams within a sports league.

contract–an agreement to play for a certain team.

debut–first appearance.

draft–a system that allows teams to acquire new players coming into a league.

expansion team–a new team that is added to an existing league.

favorite–the person or team that is expected to win.

free agent–a player who is not signed to a team.

general manager–an executive who runs a team and is responsible for finding and signing players.

offseason–the time of year when there are no games.

pick six–an interception returned for a touchdown.

pocket–the area behind the line of scrimmage where the quarterback stands after dropping back to pass.

Pro Bowl–a postseason competition that the NFL's all-stars are invited to compete in.

professional–a person who gets paid to perform.

retire–to end one's career.

rookie–a professional athlete in his or her first year of competition.

roster–a list of players who make up a team.

shotgun—a formation in which the quarterback lines up 5 to 7 yards behind the center and takes the snap in the air.

turnover—loss of the ball to the other team through an interception or a fumble.

upset—an unexpected victory by a supposedly weaker team or player.

veteran—someone who has played for many years.

ONLINE RESOURCES

To learn more about the Baltimore Ravens, please visit **abdobooklinks.com** or scan this QR code. These links are routinely monitored and updated to provide the most current information available.

INDEX